Francis Frith's
AROUND ST. IVES

PHOTOGRAPHIC MEMORIES

Francis Frith's
AROUND ST. IVES

◆

Des Hannigan

FRITH
BOOK CO

First published in the United Kingdom in 1999 by
Frith Book Company Ltd

Text and Design copyright © Frith Book Company Ltd
Photographs copyright © The Francis Frith Collection

The Frith photographs and the Frith logo are reproduced under licence from Heritage
Photographic Resources Ltd, the owners of the Frith archive and trademarks

British Library Cataloguing in Publication Data

Around St Ives
Des Hannigan
ISBN 1-85937-068-3

Frith Book Company Ltd
Frith's Barn, Teffont,
Salisbury, Wiltshire SP3 5QP
Tel: +44 (0) 1722 716 376
Email: frithbook.co.uk

Printed and bound in Great Britain

CONTENTS

FRANCIS FRITH: *Victorian Pioneer*

FRANCIS FRITH, Victorian founder of the world-famous photographic archive, was a complex and multitudinous man. A devout Quaker and a highly successful Victorian businessman, he was both philosophic by nature and pioneering in outlook.

By 1855 Francis Frith had already established a wholesale grocery business in Liverpool, and sold it for the astonishing sum of £200,000, which is the equivalent today of over £15,000,000. Now a multi-millionaire, he was able to indulge his passion for travel. As a child he had pored over travel books written by early explorers, and his fancy and imagination had been stirred by family holidays to the sublime mountain regions of Wales and Scotland. 'What a land of spirit-stirring and enriching scenes and places!' he had written. He was to return to these scenes of grandeur in later years to 'recapture the thousands of vivid and tender memories', but with a different purpose. Now in his thirties, and captivated by the new science of photography, Frith set out on a series of pioneering journeys to the Nile regions that occupied him from 1856 until 1860.

INTRIGUE AND ADVENTURE

He took with him on his travels a specially-designed wicker carriage that acted as both dark-room and sleeping chamber. These far-flung journeys were packed with intrigue and adventure. In his life story, written when he was sixty-three, Frith tells of being held captive by bandits, and of fighting 'an awful midnight battle to the very point of surrender with a deadly pack of hungry, wild dogs'. Sporting flowing Arab costume, Frith arrived at Akaba by camel seventy years before Lawrence, where he encountered 'desert princes and rival sheikhs, blazing with jewel-hilted swords'.

During these extraordinary adventures he was assiduously exploring the desert regions bordering the Nile and patiently recording the antiquities and peoples with his camera. He was the first photographer to venture beyond the sixth cataract. Africa was still the mysterious 'Dark Continent', and Stanley and Livingstone's historic meeting was a decade into the future. The conditions for picture taking confound belief. He laboured for hours in his wicker dark-room in the sweltering heat of the desert, while the volatile chemicals fizzed dangerously in their trays. Often he was forced to work in remote tombs and caves where conditions were cooler. Back in London he exhibited his photographs and was 'rapturously cheered' by members of the Royal Society. His reputation as a photographer was made overnight. An eminent modern historian has likened their impact on the population of the time to that on our own generation of the first photographs taken on the surface of the moon.

VENTURE OF A LIFE-TIME

Characteristically, Frith quickly spotted the opportunity to create a new business as a specialist publisher of photographs. He lived in an era of immense and sometimes violent change. For the poor in the early part of Victoria's reign work was a drudge and the hours long, and people had precious little free time to enjoy themselves.

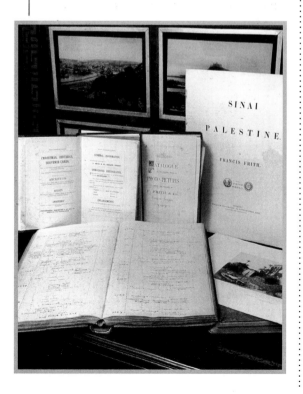

Most had no transport other than a cart or gig at their disposal, and had not travelled far beyond the boundaries of their own town or village. However, by the 1870s, the railways had threaded their way across the country, and Bank Holidays and half-day Saturdays had been made obligatory by Act of Parliament. All of a sudden the ordinary working man and his family were able to enjoy days out and see a little more of the world.

With characteristic business acumen, Francis Frith foresaw that these new tourists would enjoy having souvenirs to commemorate their days out. In 1860 he married Mary Ann Rosling and set out with the intention of photographing every city, town and village in Britain. For the next thirty years he travelled the country by train and by pony and trap, producing fine photographs of seaside resorts and beauty spots that were keenly bought by millions of Victorians. These prints were painstakingly pasted into family albums and pored over during the dark nights of winter, rekindling precious memories of summer excursions.

THE RISE OF FRITH & CO

Frith's studio was soon supplying retail shops all over the country. To meet the demand he gathered about him a small team of photographers, and published the work of independent artist-photographers of the calibre of Roger Fenton and Francis Bedford. In order to gain some understanding of the scale of Frith's business one only has to look at the catalogue issued by Frith & Co in 1886: it runs to some 670

pages, listing not only many thousands of views of the British Isles but also many photographs of most European countries, and China, Japan, the USA and Canada – note the sample page shown above from the hand-written *Frith & Co* ledgers detailing pictures taken. By 1890 Frith had created the greatest specialist photographic publishing company in the world, with over 2,000 outlets – more than the combined number that Boots and WH Smith have today! The picture on the right shows the *Frith & Co* display board at Ingleton in the Yorkshire Dales. Beautifully constructed with mahogany frame and gilt inserts, it could display up to a dozen local scenes.

POSTCARD BONANZA

The ever-popular holiday postcard we know today took many years to develop. In 1870 the Post Office issued the first plain cards, with a pre-printed stamp on one face. In 1894 they allowed other publishers' cards to be sent through the mail with an attached adhesive halfpenny stamp. Demand grew rapidly, and in 1895 a new size of postcard was permitted called the

court card, but there was little room for illustration. In 1899, a year after Frith's death, a new card measuring 5.5 x 3.5 inches became the standard format, but it was not until 1902 that the divided back came into being, with address and message on one face and a full-size illustration on the other. *Frith & Co* were in the vanguard of postcard development, and Frith's sons Eustace and Cyril continued their father's monumental task, expanding the number of views offered to the public and recording more and more places in Britain, as the coasts and countryside were opened up to mass travel.

Francis Frith died in 1898 at his villa in Cannes, his great project still growing. The archive he created continued in business for another seventy years. By 1970 it contained over a third of a million pictures of 7,000 cities, towns and villages. The massive photographic record Frith has left to us stands as a living monument to a special and very remarkable man.

Frith's Archive: *A Unique Legacy*

FRANCIS FRITH'S legacy to us today is of immense significance and value, for the magnificent archive of evocative photographs he created provides a unique record of change in 7,000 cities, towns and villages throughout Britain over a century and more. Frith and his fellow studio photographers revisited locations many times down the years to update their views, compiling for us an enthralling and colourful pageant of British life and character.

We tend to think of Frith's sepia views of Britain as nostalgic, for most of us use them to conjure up memories of places in our own lives with which we have family associations. It often makes us forget that to Francis Frith they were records of daily life as it was actually being lived in the cities, towns and villages of his day. The Victorian age was one of great and often bewildering change for ordinary people, and though the pictures evoke an impression of slower times, life was as busy and hectic as it is today.

We are fortunate that Frith was a photographer of the people, dedicated to recording the minutiae of everyday life. For it is this sheer wealth of visual data, the painstaking chronicle of changes in dress, transport, street layouts, buildings, housing, engineering and landscape that captivates us so much today. His remarkable images offer us a powerful link with the past and with the lives of our ancestors.

TODAY'S TECHNOLOGY

Computers have now made it possible for Frith's many thousands of images to be accessed almost instantly. In the Frith archive today, each photograph is carefully 'digitised' then stored on a CD Rom. Frith archivists can locate a single photograph amongst thousands within seconds. Views can be catalogued and sorted under a variety of categories of place and content to the immediate benefit of researchers. Inexpensive reference prints can be created for them at the touch of a mouse button, and a wide range of books and other printed materials assembled and published for a wider, more general readership - in the next twelve months over a hundred Frith local history titles will be published! The day-to-day workings of the archive are very different from how they were in Francis Frith's time: imagine the herculean task of sorting through eleven tons of glass negatives as Frith had to do to locate a particular sequence of pictures! Yet the archive still prides itself on maintaining the same high standards of excellence laid down by Francis Frith, including the painstaking cataloguing and indexing of every view.

It is curious to reflect on how the internet now allows researchers in America and elsewhere greater instant access to the archive than Frith himself ever enjoyed. Many thousands of individual views can be called up on screen within seconds on one of the Frith internet sites, enabling people living continents away to revisit the streets of their ancestral home town, or view places in Britain where they have enjoyed holidays. Many overseas researchers welcome the chance to view special theme selections, such as transport, sports, costume and ancient monuments.

We are certain that Francis Frith would have heartily approved of these modern developments, for he himself was always working at the very limits of Victorian photographic technology.

THE VALUE OF THE ARCHIVE TODAY

Because of the benefits brought by the computer, Frith's images are increasingly studied by social historians, by researchers into genealogy and ancestory, by architects, town planners, and by teachers and schoolchildren involved in local history projects. In addition, the archive offers every one of us a unique opportunity to examine the places where we and our families have lived and worked down the years. Immensely successful in Frith's own era, the archive is now, a century and more on, entering a new phase of popularity.

THE PAST IN TUNE WITH THE FUTURE

Historians consider the Francis Frith Collection to be of prime national importance. It is the only archive of its kind remaining in private ownership and has been valued at a million pounds. However, this figure is now rapidly increasing as digital technology enables more and more people around the world to enjoy its benefits.

Francis Frith's archive is now housed in an historic timber barn in the beautiful village of Teffont in Wiltshire. Its founder would not recognize the archive office as it is today. In place of the many thousands of dusty boxes containing glass plate negatives and an all-pervading odour of photographic chemicals, there are now ranks of computer screens. He would be amazed to watch his images travelling round the world at unimaginable speeds through network and internet lines.

The archive's future is both bright and exciting. Francis Frith, with his unshakeable belief in making photographs available to the greatest number of people, would undoubtedly approve of what is being done today with his lifetime's work. His photographs, depicting our shared past, are now bringing pleasure and enlightenment to millions around the world a century and more after his death.

St. Ives – *An Introduction*

The famous Cornish resort of St Ives is loved by tens of thousands of visitors for its superb beaches, its narrow cobbled streets and courtyards, its glittering sea and clear air and for its friendly hospitable people. Like all of West Cornwall, St Ives seems more like a slice of the Mediterranean; yet it remains reassuringly British. Within the maze-like streets of the town's harbour area and in the ruggedness of its adjoining coastline lies the story of a colourful past that has forged the unique character of the St Ives of today.

The town is named after St Ia, one of a number of Irish 'missionaries' who came to Cornwall and Wales during the 5th and 6th centuries, a time when trade and cultural influences flowed from Ireland into Western Britain. St Ia is said to have been a holy woman, a princess, or the daughter of an Irish chieftain. There are tall tales of how a number of Irish 'saints' sailed to Britain in baskets, sea shells, even perched miraculously upon floating millstones. St Ia is said to have sailed across the Irish sea on a leaf, but her voyage was more likely to have been made in a seaworthy coracle-type vessel constructed of leaf-like, layered hides. Legend and folk tale

embroidered later stories. To this day ivy leaves are a feature of the St Ives coat of arms, although this symbol may in turn have originated as a punning reference to the already established name of 'Ives'.

St Ia probably landed near the island-like promontory that is such a striking feature of St Ives today. The promontory was known originally as Pendinas, 'headland of the fortification', and may have been the site of a defended trading centre from as early as the Bronze Age. Known simply as The Island, though it is not an island in the defined sense, the headland is a cherished symbol of old St. Ives. The Island has remained an open space to this day because it was used traditionally for mending fishing nets and for drying washing. It is referred to by true-born St Ives people as 'The Island', but never as St Ives Island. The Chapel of St Nicholas stands on top of The Island. Originally medieval, it was a seamen's chapel and once displayed a light to guide incoming vessels to harbour. The building was also a customs lookout and a pilots' watch house in its time. It was commandeered by the War Office at the end of the 19th century, and in 1904 the authorities planned to demolish the building. Fierce local opposition to the plan saved the chapel. Today the building is still used for occasional services.

FISHING

The settlement that developed on the sandy isthmus between The Island and the mainland became known as Porthia, then as Sancte Ye, Seynt Iysse and finally St Ives. For centuries the settlement survived on fishing. Vast shoals of pilchard, herring and mackerel teemed through the shallow waters of the bay

church of St Ia. The granite used for the church was quarried from coastal cliffs near Zennor four miles to the west and was carried to St Ives aboard boats and barges when sea conditions were calm. By 1488 the town had its own market and held two annual fairs. In 1588 St. Ives became a Parliamentary borough, one of the most infamous 'rotten boroughs' of the time. It returned two MPs on the back of enthusiastic bribery and corruption. A first charter was granted to the town in 1639. This charter was withdrawn by James II in 1682 because St Ives, like other independ-

and sustained St Ives as a fishing port throughout the Middle Ages and into the early part of the 20th century. The settlement grew into a thriving township during the late 14th century after the once busy seaport of Lelant on the nearby Hayle Estuary became heavily silted with sand, as well as with the mud that was washed down from the medieval copper and tin mines of the surrounding countryside.

The early 15th century saw St Ives gaining religious independence from Lelant because of the building of the town's handsome

ent-minded towns, resisted the king's attempts to exercise more control over its affairs. The charter was reinstated in 1685; after this St Ives became firmly established as a successful and self-confident market town.

Throughout the 18th and early 19th centuries the town flourished in isolation from the rest of the West Country. Fishing, especially for pilchard, was the mainstay of St Ives during the 19th century. At one time nearly 800 men and boys were employed in the fishery and 400 boats took part. Virtually the entire shore-based population was involved in handling and processing the fish and in the related industries of rope and net-making, net-mending and shipbuilding. Along the adjacent coastline towards Carbis Bay and

Wesley established a tenacious religious tradition that united the fishing and mining communities during the 18th century. Methodism remains a strong element in the life of St Ives

inland from the harbour, tin and copper mining was a strong part of the local economy.

DIVIDED

St Ives became physically and socially divided into 'Downalong', the lower harbour area of 'old' St Ives that was populated mainly by fishing families, and 'Upalong', the higher inland district where copper and tin mining dominated lives and landscape. The rivalry between the two districts was intense. In keeping with such lively diversity strong debate still engulfs the proper use of the words Downalong and Upalong. The spoken versions of 'Down'long' and 'Up'long' are still considered 'proper' usage by true-born St Ives people today even in written form.

The inward-looking world of old St Ives proved fertile ground for the powerful religious beliefs of Methodism. The inspirational nonconformist preachers Charles and John

today, although divisions amongst Methodists in the past have given rise to the establishing of independent religious foundations.

GOLDEN AGE

St. Ives' golden age lasted for the first thirty or so years of the 19th century; later, mining and fishing declined through a sequence of increasingly threadbare periods of boom and bust. As late as the 1890s, however, hundreds of tons of fish were still being sent off by train and the pilchard and herring seasons were still key elements in St Ives' life until the 1930s. The town's splendid sailing vessels that were used for both fishing and cargo-carrying were slow to convert to the new form of steam propulsion; as the core industries and their dependent trades declined, many townsfolk emigrated or moved to other parts of Cornwall and Britain.

In 1877, the economy of St Ives was boosted by the building of a scenic branch railway to the town from St Erth on the main Penzance line. The railway rejuvenated the fishing trade by opening up distant markets, but the future lay with the fast-developing tourist industry. Victorian tourists were soon attracted to St Ives, and from the late 19th century onwards the railway brought more and more holidaymakers to the town. The new craze for sea bathing encouraged tourism even more, and the once neglected and rubbish-strewn beaches were cleaned up and given over to bathing huts and to recreation. Soon the sands recovered their famous golden colour as the decline of seagoing industry continued.

Tourism flourished from the late 19th century onwards, and coincided with the arrival of influential artists such as the American James McNeill Whistler and the German-born Walter Sickert. English painters later brought to St Ives the outdoors, or plein air, style of painting that they had learnt in France. They found in St Ives the subject matter and the clear accurate light that suited the plein air style. Today at the St Ives Tate Gallery, a striking building above the town's magnificent Porthmeor Beach, the celebration of that artistic tradition helps sustain St Ives' thriving tourist industry.

CORNISH CHARACTER

Today, St Ives has retained its richly Cornish character, especially in the Down'long harbour-side area. Here, narrow cobbled streets and alleyways dappled with sun and shade weave their charming way amidst rough-walled granite cottages and houses, art galleries, craft-markets, colourful pubs and restaurants. Fishing and its associated industries no longer dominate the quays, courts and alleyways of Down'long, although Smeaton's Pier, the main quay of the harbour,

is still the preserve of St Ives' fishing community and is the place where fish are landed and where nets are mended.

Over the years, St Ives has spread beyond its original sea-centred heart, and the wider borough now includes the mainly residential villages of Carbis Bay and Lelant on the southern arm of St Ives Bay. The Bay is a magnificent setting, and today has some of the finest holiday beaches in Europe. Sparkling seas, exhilarating surf and shining sand are the themes. Much spectacular colour is added to St. Ives in the summer months by the famous floral displays that have won international awards.

As well as the Tate Gallery, the town's many other galleries add to the general quality and pleasure of the St Ives artistic experience, as does the September Festival, a two-week celebration of Arts and Music. There is also an excellent town museum at Wheal Dream, just north of Smeaton's Pier.

Within the modern St Ives, with its bustling tourism, its network of arts and craft galleries and gift shops, its fine restaurants and pubs, its beach culture and its inescapable 'quaintness', there survives an intensely Cornish town. The character of old St Ives, captured vividly in paintings and in old photographs, reflects a vigorous and colourful past that has relevance still in the very different world of today.

The Old Town (Down'long)

DOWNALONG, or Down'long in its popular form, is the hallowed name used for old St Ives at its most authentic by born and bred St Ives people. Down'long is defined roughly as the area of granite cottages, houses and other buildings that surrounds the harbour and that straddles the neck of land between the high promontory of The Island and the inland parts of the town. Within this area lie numerous streets and alleyways that wriggle to and fro like granite canyons between the buildings. Behind Wharf Road is the narrow cobbled Fore Street, Down'long's only main thoroughfare before Wharf Road was built in 1922. Today Fore Street is thronged with holidaymakers in summer and is often as busy in winter. Here are numerous art galleries and shops of all types including those selling standard goods as well as craft work and gifts.

To the west of Fore Street is the heart of Down'long, an enchanting maze of alleyways and courtyards with fascinating names such as The Digey, Teetotal Street, Love Lane, Virgin Street and Mount Zion. They lead to The Island, and to Barnoon, a higher part of the old town above Porthmeor Beach. Around the Digey area is where the town's oldest buildings survive and where the real flavour of St Ives can be enjoyed. In numerous courtyards and open-sided cellars, where flowers blossom amidst colourful paint work and golden granite, pilchards and herring were once laid out or 'baulked' into carefully arranged piles, the layers of fish being separated by layers of salt. The combined weight forced oil out of the fish. The oil drained along channels in the stone floors and then into granite containers. It was used for numerous purposes including lighting.

Much of the fish salted in this way was then packed into hogshead barrels and shipped to Mediterranean countries, to Catholic Italy especially, where a religious ban on eating meat on Fridays and during Lent ensured a huge market for Cornish fish. As well as the pressing, and then the packing of fish into barrels, St Ives was once noted for its smoked herring, or 'kippers', whose preparation in smoke houses added to the miasma of smells and vapours. A Victorian visitor once remarked famously that the overpowering stench was enough to stop the town clock.

Near the south entrance to Fore Street stands the old Market House, a free-standing building of 1832 that replaced the original of 1490. Running west from the Market House is the High Street. Opposite the Market House is the parish church of St Ia, its handsome granite tower red-gold in the sunlight against blue skies. The cool quiet interior of the church is graced with a carved wagon roof of great style and by equally handsome bench ends. South of the church beyond St Andrew's Street is the charming area of The Warren and Pedn Olva, an area that bridges the gap between Down'long and the lovely Porthminster Beach, which fits within the definition of old St. Ives.

NORWAY LANE 1890 23022
Part of this typical old lane was demolished in the 1930s; the cleared area eventually became a car park. The residents were rehoused in council estates on the slopes above the town.

BETHESDA HILL 1890 24185
This photograph clearly shows the crowded masts of St. Ives' fishing boats in the harbour. There were over 400 boats working from St. Ives during the 19th century heyday of its fishing.

OLD HOUSES 1890 24186

This area of Down'long near the present day Mariners' Church at Norway Square has changed considerably since this photograph was taken over 100 years ago. The cottage on the left has been replaced with gardens; the wall on the right was once used as a place where slaughtered pigs were scalded and skinned.

BACK ROAD WEST 1890 24187

This road still exists and leads to Porthmeor Beach and to today's St Ives Tate Gallery. The cottages are typical fishermen's homes of the time; the stairs led to living quarters, while the ground floors were the fish cellars and boat stores.

BACK ROAD EAST
1890

This view looks towards Back Road West. (St Ives' streets were often named with commendable simplicity). This picture again shows the upper living quarters and ground floor fish cellars typical of the time.

—◆—

BUNKERS HILL
1892

This street is now bedecked with flower baskets, but the splendidly cut granite blocks and steps of the houses still survive, as do the cobbles, or 'setts', of the street's surface.

BACK ROAD EAST 1890 24189

BUNKERS HILL 1892 29872

BARROW HILL 1898 41612
A view down the hill towards the fine tower of the Parish Church of St Ia. The first building on the left was a Navigation School at the time. It was demolished in 1910 to make way for an early cinema, The Picturedrome.

FORE STREET 1906 56540
Fore Street is still one of St Ives' busiest thoroughfares. This view shows the street furniture of the time; on the right is a gas lamp and on the left sturdy 'spur stones' that were placed at street corners to stop wagon wheels from scraping the walls.

NORWAY LANE 1906 56544
Note the deep gully in the street. This was for rainwater drainage, and would also have carried off waste water from fish cellars.

THE DIGEY 1906 56546

THE DIGEY
1906

This photograph shows the Digey with a rare collection of children and cats. The name 'Digey' is thought by some to derive from the Cornish for meadow. Another derivation may be 'Dye Chy', a reference to a dyeing house, which was once located in the area; the Cornish 'chy' means house.

◆

BAILEY'S LANE
1906

A charming older name for the lane was the fascinating 'Street-petite'. The young man holding the wheelbarrow worked for a local grocer and used the barrow for delivering goods, or, as can be seen here, for giving a local youngster a jaunt.

BAILEY'S LANE 1906 56545

CAPEL COURT 1906 56547
A very old part of St. Ives. This area is next to the present day Sloop Inn. Left of the building is Pudding Bag Lane,
so called because like a pudding bag it had only one opening. House and lane were demolished in the 1930s.

WHARF ROAD 1906 56550
This view looks up towards Pier View. On the right is part of the Marine Dealers' Stores run by the famous St Ives 'naive' painter Alfred Wallis. Works of Wallis's can be seen at the St Ives Tate Gallery.

A QUAINT CORNER 1906 56551

This photograph, taken from the harbour side, shows the old buildings that stood where the present amusement arcade is now located. The lane links the harbour front with Fore Street. The buildings on the right were badly damaged by a fierce fire in 1970.

ST PETER'S STREET 1906 56552
There is a typical wall-mounted gas lamp of the time. Such lamps were often removed during the summer months and were often left unlit on moonlit nights in winter, an impressive example of early civic cost-cutting.

BUNKERS HILL AND NORWAY LANE 1905 56553
The building on the right was later replaced by another. The gap leading off to the right between the buildings is
Norway Lane.

BACK ROAD EAST 1906 56548
Here a local fisherman enjoys a quiet pipe on the steps and two local boys lounge at the entrance to the fish cellar where pilchards were processed, or 'cured'.

FORE STREET 1922 72852
Compared with the photograph of Fore Street in 1906, the gas lamp is still in place, but the corner is now plastered with adverts for the cinema on Barnoon Hill.

DICK'S HILL 1922 72855

A view down Fish Street, known also as Dick's Hill, looking towards the harbour. The view is very different today. All of the buildings lying downhill from where the mats are drying on the wall were demolished in the 1920s and 1930s.

VIRGIN STREET 1927 80065
St Ives is still famous for its cats. In the fishing era, every household had at least one cat, for the very practical purpose of keeping the net cellars free of mice. Natural fibre nets of that time were damaged by mice nibbling at them.

WASHING DAY 1927 80066
A classic washing-day scene in St. Peter's Street Court, known also as Luke's Court. The tap at the top of the steps was shared by most of the surrounding households.

BETHESDA HILL 1927 80068

One explanation given for the name Bethesda is that the street had five porches and at the bottom of the street lay a 'pool', the harbour. This all fitted the New Testament description of the Pool of Bethesda and its surroundings in Jerusalem.

WILLS LANE c1960 S22122
A more modern view of St Ives, with flower boxes gracing the windows of the houses and with smart whitewashed walls. Today, there is a very fine art gallery here, the Wills Lane Gallery.

The Harbour

THE HEART of St Ives is its picturesque harbour where fishing boats still bob on the tide. The harbour is sheltered from westerly and northerly winds by Smeaton's Pier, built in 1770 to the design of John Smeaton, the great engineer responsible for the original Eddystone Lighthouse, which is now reconstructed on the famous Hoe at Plymouth. An attractive lighthouse was added to Smeaton's Pier in 1831. Plans for an outer harbour led to the building in the 1860s of a mainly wooden pier to the north of Smeaton's Pier. This structure could not withstand the battering of north-easterly gales and was soon destroyed. The wooden stumps can still be seen today. In 1890, a more substantial granite extension, the 'Victoria Extension', was added to Smeaton's Pier. At its seaward end a cast-iron lighthouse was built. Today, 'Smeaton's Pier', as the entire pier is still known, retains the granite character of the original.

On the south side of the harbour opposite Smeaton's Pier a shorter quay known as West Pier was built in 1894. At the entrance to West Pier stands the modern lifeboat house, a constant reminder of St Ives' great tradition of lifesaving at sea. Because of the tidal nature of St Ives harbour, the lifeboat is kept on a wheeled cradle. When the lifeboat is called out at high tide this cradle is manoeuvred by tractor down a slipway directly into the water. At low tide the cradle is taken across the sand and is pushed into the sea to where the water is deep enough for the lifeboat to float. The procedure is easily viewed from Wharf Road and is always an impressive sight.

Until 1922 the harbour beach extended nearly to the walls of the seaward houses of St Ives. Then Wharf Road was built alongside the harbour sands. It ran from West Pier to link with The Wharf and Quay Street and with Smeaton's Pier. Today, Wharf Road and its continuation of The Wharf are busy thoroughfares from which there are wide views across the harbour into St Ives Bay.

The popular image of St Ives today is a sanitised one that is far removed from the lively realities of past industry. In the heyday of fishing and commerce a hundred or so years ago the streets of Down'long stank with the smell of fish and domestic waste, and the harbour sands were stained and strewn with the muck from coal ships and merchant carriers and with the detritus of the fishing industry.

Where pleasure boats, yachts and modern fishing vessels now lie the harbour was once crowded with characteristic St Ives 'luggers', the dark-sailed, sturdy wooden vessels used in the drift net fishery. Larger merchant ships unloaded everything from foodstuffs to coal onto horse-drawn carts on the harbour foreshore, and fish were gutted on the beach and were laid out for sale. Those days are long gone, but the harbour of today remains a memorable, lively place for residents and visitors alike.

SMEATON'S PIER 1890 24176
Lines of Cornish 'luggers', the characteristic sail-powered vessels of the St Ives fishing industry, lie in packed tiers on the harbour sand. The quay side is piled high with fish boxes.

THE HARBOUR 1890 24177
The boat in the foreground is a typical St Ives 'gig'. Its shallow keel was specially suited to a tidal harbour like St Ives. Beyond the fishing boats can be seen the prow of a cargo vessel.

THE LIFEBOATMEN 1906 56543
The record of St Ives' lifeboats is an outstanding one, but has meant great sacrifice. Seven of the eight-man crew of the lifeboat 'John and Sarah Eliza Stych' were lost in a terrible disaster in 1939 when the lifeboat was wrecked near Godrevy Island.

THE WHARF
1890 24184

The road is very different to its modern
counterpart, and reflects how much the sea was
the main way out of St Ives. Cars pass by today
where boats were once pulled up on the beach.

THE OLD SLOOP INN
1906 56541
On the immediate right is the entrance to the
long since demolished Pudding Bag Lane.
Further right is the entrance to Fish Street.

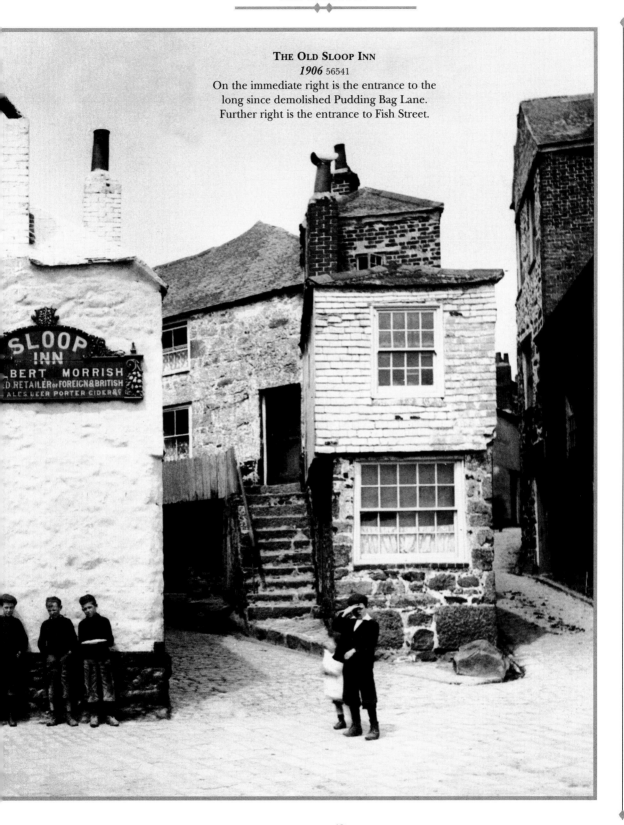

THE HARBOUR 1908 61074A
Fishing boats lie at their moorings on the left, while a small cargo carrier lies moored just off the beach. Horses and carts were still the best way of loading and off-loading in a tidal harbour.

PILCHARD BOATS 1908 61076
These splendid vessels were used in the drift net fishery that involved setting lengths of net just below the sea's surface. The older method of seine netting involved smaller vessels setting a very large net with which they encircled a large shoal of fish close to the beach.

NEW WHARF ROAD 1922 72831
This view shows The Promenade, or the New Wharf Road as it was also known, before railings and pavements were added. The broken walls midway along the line of buildings were ruins left after a fire of 1915.

THE HARBOUR 1925 78655
A classic harbour scene taken at low tide. Large numbers of gulls gathered in the harbour even in those days, but unlike today's gulls, many of which nest on St Ives' rooftops, these gulls returned at night to nesting colonies on the sea cliffs along the coast.

THE HARBOUR
1925 78658
Fish being gutted on the harbour beach, long before modern hygiene laws came into play. The horse-drawn cart was a common mode of transporting fish from the beach.

THE FISH MARKET 1925 78659

The busy fish market on The Wharf. The wooden building on the railed platform is Shore Shelter Lodge, one of the famous St Ives Fishermen's 'Lodges', where fishermen gathered in their spare time. It is one of only three lodges still in existence.

SMEATON'S PIER 1925 78666

SMEATON'S PIER
1925
This photograph shows the old lighthouse of 1831 in the background. The fishermen are checking their lobster pots, the 'inkwell' shape of which has not changed to this day.

◆

WESTCOTT'S QUAY
1927
This view shows Westcott's Quay before Pednolver Walk, popularly known as Lambeth Walk, was built above the beach in the 1930s to mask a drainage system that led to large holding tanks further along The Wharf. The building on the left no longer exists.

WESTCOTT'S QUAY 1927 80064

THE HARBOUR
1926 78664
Gulls have always haunted St Ives harbour,
although today they scavenge food refuse rather
than the offal from fish gutting and cleaning. In
this photograph a flock of gulls home in on
unattended fish.

THE SLOOP INN AND SLIPWAY c1955 S22028

A view from the harbour with the Sloop Inn at the centre of the picture and with Fish Street leading uphill to the right. This photograph illustrates the more prosperous look to St Ives' harbourside buildings compared with 50 years before.

WESTCOTT'S QUAY c1955 S22034

Pednolver Walk, or 'Lambeth Walk', leading from Westcott's Quay to Wharf Road. This view shows the narrow promenade without its railings, which were added in a later more safety-conscious age.

THE HARBOUR C1955 S22089
Wharf Road is now a busy thoroughfare, the harbour wall a sturdy granite breakwater crowned with iron railings and tall street lamps. The days when boats were pulled up on the foreshore almost as far as the front doors of the houses are long gone.

THE PROMENADE C1960 S22121
St Ives as a holiday town in the 1960s, with cafes and restaurants. The fishing connection survives, however. Boats still dominate the harbour at low tide and signs advertise lobster and crab.

WHARF ROAD c1960 S22131

St Ives harbourside is crowded with holidaymakers, at a time when the town was probably at its peak as a tourist destination. Billboards for the popular Cornish Belle cruises reflect a changed world for St Ives seagoers.

THE HARBOUR c1960 S22187

This view shows Pednolver Walk, (Lambeth Walk), its railings now firmly in place, and groups of holidaymakers enjoying the Cornish sunshine. The building flanking the walk has the characteristic rough stone work of old St Ives.

THE HARBOUR c1960 S22132
This view shows a number of St. Ives gigs, small shallow-keeled boats. As the tide fell and the water in the harbour drained away, the gigs' shallow keels allowed them more time for getting into the harbour than the bigger deep-keeled fishing boat in the background.

PREPARING THE BAIT c1960 S22161
Skate and ray wings were often hung up to dry. These fish exuded a great deal of slime and ammonia, but properly treated and prepared they made a tasty dish. The large pot, made out of willow wands, was probably used for keeping crabs, crayfish and lobsters alive underwater until taken to market.

The Beaches

THE BEACHES of St Ives are the town's crowning glories. Seen as convenient landing places if position and prevailing weather allowed, these now 'golden' shores were once maritime industrial sites. Victorian tourism transformed popular perceptions of the seaside at the same time as traditional seagoing industries, such as fishing and cargo carrying, declined.

The town's beaches were once bustling work places. Today they are major tourist venues, and the inspiration for numerous artists. They are, in many ways, the real focus of St Ives as a holiday resort, although the vagaries of British weather and the huge growth in cheap holidays abroad have led to diversity in the tourism culture of the town. Still considered 'the best in the west' by St Ives people and by devoted holidaymakers, the town's beaches offer a choice of facilities to suit everyone.

The main beaches of Porthmeor and Porthminster, known affectionately by locals as 'Meor' and 'Minster', are extremely well managed. Porthmeor Beach lies on the western edge of the town and is more open to the impact of the Atlantic. It is an exhilarating beach, famous for its powerful surf, yet it is also an enjoyable traditional venue where holidaymakers who are not attracted by surfing or body-boarding can soak up the sun, or just dip their toes in the curling edge of foaming waves. The beach is a regular winner of the Keep Britain Tidy Group's Blue Flag Award for overall excellence. Its golden sands run up against a line of buildings that once accommodated net lofts and boat stores. Many of the net lofts were converted to artists' studios when their traditional use declined. Their spaciousness, and the large windows that captured the clear northern light, were an ideal combination for the painter. Perched above and behind the beach is the St Ives Tate Gallery; it contains an absorbing collection of works by 20th-century St Ives artists. The view of Porthmeor Beach from the gallery's top floor patio is breathtaking.

Porthminster Beach lies on the eastern edge of St Ives within the sheltering arms of the inner bay; its seas are less vigorous than those of Porthmeor, its air is more placid. Porthminster is an ideal beach for families. It is very well maintained and is another regular winner of awards. In the great days of the pilchard fishing industry, nets were set offshore by skilfully manoeuvred boats until the vast shoal of fish was encircled like a silver pool. When the industry declined and tourism grew, the broken hulks of seine net boats lay above the beach, their timbers rotting until they were finally cleared away, signalling the sad end of an era.

As if two such magnificent beaches were not enough, St Ives boasts its Harbour Beach, within stepping distance of Wharf Road and the busy heart of the town. Between here and Porthmeor Beach and within the shadow of The Island, lies the much smaller Porthgwidden, or 'Gwidden', Beach, a surprising little venue that captures perfectly the 'Mediterranean' ambience of Cornish St. Ives.

ON THE BEACH
1890 24178
This delightful scene shows a group of youngsters enjoying the harbour beach. Behind them are classic St Ives fishing boats, known as luggers because the type of sail they used was called a lug sail. The children were probably on a school outing or Sunday School 'tea treat'.

FROM COASTGUARD 1890 24172

THE ISLAND 1890 24180A

FROM COASTGUARD
1890

This panoramic view of Porthminster beach and St. Ives was taken from near the local coastguard station. On the left of the picture pilchard boats can be seen drawn up at the top of the beach.

◆

THE ISLAND
1890

This view looks towards The Island. Wind and tide can build up or deplete sand on Cornish beaches. There is plenty of sand at Porthmeor today, and there are numerous facilities for the modern holidaymaker.

PORTHMINSTER BEACH 47677A
Holiday time at the beginning of the 19th century. The meeting of two worlds is illustrated by the seine net boats still drawn up on the sand. Fishing in this form was to continue in tandem with tourism until the 1930s.

PORTHMEOR BEACH 1908 61080A
This view shows the beach complete with bathing tents. Only a few years earlier, in 1899, the local council had been criticised for allowing the dumping of ash from the nearby gas works onto the beach.

PORTHMEOR BEACH
1922

There are more bathing tents; by now the St Ives' beaches were being managed as tourist attractions. In the distance can be seen a slipway that was built from The Island to Porthmeor Beach in 1911.

PORTHMINSTER BEACH AND ISLAND
1925

Compared with the view of Porthminster Beach taken in 1890, this view indicates how much the holiday industry had taken over the St Ives beaches. Bathing tents effectively close off the beach, and the number of seine net boats has dwindled.

PORTHMEOR BEACH 1922 72843

PORTHMINSTER BEACH AND ISLAND 1925 78640

PEDN OLVA 1925 78649

This low tide view shows the rocky promontory of Pedn Olva that lies between Porthminster Beach and the foreshore up to West Pier. Foreshore houses in St. Ives were built with tall gables, and had few ground-floor windows on the seaward side.

PEDN OLVA 1930 83337

Pedn Olva headland pictured on a quiet summer's day and viewed from its more picturesque Porthminster Beach side. Moored fishing boats enhance the idyllic scene. There is still a popular hotel on the headland today.

PORTHMINSTER BEACH
1925 78646
The public has not yet abandoned Victorian modesty when it comes to bathing costumes, and not many people seem to be eager to swim, but deck-chairs and buckets and spades are well established.

PORTHMINSTER BEACH c1955 S22013
This photograph was taken during the heyday of mass tourism. The tea house, which still functions today as a delightful cafe-restaurant, stands at the near end of the beach. There are no surviving traces of the once major industry of seine net fishing.

SMEATON'S PIER c1955 S22033
Looking across the sands to Smeaton's Pier. Fishing boats still bob at anchor on the high tide, but tourism is now the dominant industry.

ON THE BEACH c1900 S22505

Small boats and small boys enjoy the sun. Of the buildings behind the beach, three were public houses. The central building is the famous Sloop Inn, still operating today. On the left is the former Globe and on the right the former White Hart.

PORTHGWIDDEN BEACH c1960 S22221

This view shows St Ives' smallest beach bursting at the seams at a time when beach holidays were at the height of their popularity. Behind lies The Island, crowned by the Chapel of St. Nicholas on the left, the Coastguard Lookout on the right.

The Town and Surroundings

THE HEART of St Ives is still the Down'long harbour area, but the town is much more than this. Throughout the years the town expanded inland as the sea became less of a 'road' out of St Ives; the town became ever more closely linked to its own district of Penwith and then to the rest of Cornwall and the even larger world beyond, from where an endless stream of holidaymakers came.

Throughout the later 19th century the upper parts of the town, developed as service industries, flourished as the fishing and mining communities grew. Members of the growing middle class built more comfortable homes along the higher ground that overlooked the magnificent bay. By the end of the Victorian era, substantial houses such as Draycott Terrace and Albany Terrace were established on the higher slopes. Along the main roads in and out of St. Ives, such as High Street, Tregenna Place and The Stennack, important civic and religious buildings were constructed, including the Bedford Methodist Church at the junction of High Street with Bedford Road, and St Ives Public Library on the corner of Tregenna Place and Gabriel Street.

During the second half of the 20th century the railway played a major part in developing St. Ives outside its core existence as a fishing village. The famous St Ives branch line was opened in June 1877 and for its first fifty years it carried freight and passengers; in the early 20th century freight carrying declined. Thereafter, leisure and tourism increased, not

least when the Holidays and Pay Act of 1938 launched a social revolution after the Second World War by enabling ordinary working families to enjoy annual holidays by the sea. This led to virtually the entire working population of towns such as Swindon decamping to St Ives for an annual summer holiday. The boost to tourism in the town was spectacular. In its early days of wealthy Victorian tourism the railway encouraged the development of grand hotels such as the still flourishing Porthminster and Tregenna Castle; but the railway's later role in facilitating the growth of mass tourism was probably the single greatest influence in shaping the St Ives of today.

Yet in spite of the town's development and the huge rise in its summer population during the past sixty or so years, the superb natural surroundings of St Ives have remained a delight. To the east, along the shores of Carbis Bay, a lush vegetation has created an almost park-like quality to the coast within the exhilarating curve of St Ives Bay and its distant outpost of Godrevy Lighthouse. To the west of Porthmeor Beach, beyond the rocky outcrop of Man's Head at Carrick Du and the sweeping green turf of Clodgy Point, lies a magnificent wilderness coast that runs for mile after mile towards Land's End.

It is this unique mix of holiday beach and rugged coast, modern town and ancient harbour, that has made St Ives one of the best-loved seaside resorts in Britain today.

TREGENNA CASTLE HOTEL
1890

The hotel was built as a private dwelling in the 1770s. It was converted to a hotel in 1878 by the Great Western Railway Company. Though a much modernised hotel today, the main building has changed little in external appearance.

THE BOARD SCHOOL
1890

The school was built in 1880 in The Stennack, the main road that leads out of St Ives to the west. The building was a school until 1984. It was converted into a doctor's surgery in 1992.

TREGENNA CASTLE HOTEL 1890 23023

THE BOARD SCHOOL 1890 24173

GODREVY LIGHTHOUSE 1890 24195
The lighthouse gave warning of a dangerous reef called The Stones that lies on the northern side of St Ives Bay. The lighthouse came into service in 1859 and was manned for many years, but is now automated.

THE CHAPEL OF ST NICHOLAS 1892 31161A

The Chapel was built on The Island. The original building was medieval, and was later used as a customs lookout. It was scheduled for demolition in 1904 after use by the War Office, but was preserved after strong local protest.

DRAYCOTT TERRACE 1898 41610

These houses overlook Porthminster Beach and have views of St Ives Bay that are as superb today as they were when this photograph was taken. Houses built as homes for coastguards can be seen behind them on the left.

TREGENNA PLACE 1906 56539
The handsome building on the corner, with its chateau-style turret, is the St Ives Public Library that was opened in
1897. J. Passmore Edwards, a wealthy Cornish-born newspaper proprietor, donated the money for this and for
other public buildings in Cornwall.

ALBANY TERRACE 1901 47679

The large building on the left of the picture is the present Chy an Albany Hotel. These houses, built from cut granite and with substantial bay windows, reflect a more suburban building style compared with the cottages of old St Ives.

MAN'S HEAD ROCK AND THE ISLAND 1908 61080

This view looks across the Bay to The Island from the well-named Man's Head Rock on the headland of Carrick Du. In those days the area was enjoyed by local and visitor alike, being within easy reach of the town. Man's Head Rock is just as popular today.

HIGH STREET
1922 72849
This photograph looks down the High Street towards St Ives' Parish Church. The High Street remains the main entranceway to the older part of St Ives, and is an important shopping street.

TREGENNA PLACE 1922 72850

Tregenna Place from Tregenna Hill. The narrow thoroughfare has changed little to this day, although there are many more vehicles passing to and fro.

BEDFORD ROAD METHODIST CHURCH 1922 72851
Methodists who broke from the parent society in St Ives in 1838 to form a Teetotal Society later joined the 'New Connexion' Methodists at the end of the 19th century, and moved to this neo-Gothic building.

THE CHY AN ALBANY HOTEL
1922
The Hotel is situated in Albany Terrace overlooking St Ives Bay. The hotel has a long pedigree, and has been much extended since this photograph was taken.

YORK HOUSE
1922
This imposing building is still a prominent feature of the Trenwith area of St Ives. Once a popular hotel, it is now a private nursing home.

THE CHY AN ALBANY HOTEL 1922 72853

YORK HOUSE 1922 72854

GODREVY LIGHTHOUSE 1922 73308

This dramatic lighthouse, although not named in the book as Godrevy, is said to have been the inspiration for Virginia Woolf's famous novel 'To the Lighthouse', which she wrote while staying in St Ives.

BELLAIR TERRACE 1927 80060

This fine terrace of houses is another indication of improved housing design and of the spread of St Ives onto the higher ground overlooking St Ives Bay.

THE PORTHMINSTER HOTEL 1928 81181

The Porthminster Hotel, overlooking Porthminster Beach, was opened in 1894 to accommodate the increasing number of visitors arriving in St Ives since the opening of the railway. It is now one of the town's most prestigious hotels.

THE STATION c1955 S22023

The St Erth to St Ives branch line, the last broad gauge railway to be built, was opened by the Great Western Railway in 1877. This view of the station was taken before parts of the station were sacrificed to accommodate the present station car park.

THE WARREN C1955 S22037
This narrow St Ives street got its name from a rabbit warren once situated there. The street was also used at one time as a convenient 'rope walk' where ropes were made for the fishing industry.

TREGENNA PLACE
c1955 S22085
This view shows Lake's Art and Literature Shop on the left and part of the main Post Office on the right. Tregenna Place and its continuation of the High Street are still the main thoroughfares into the harbour area of St Ives.

THE PARISH CHURCH c1955 S22084

A view looking along St Andrew's Street to the Parish Church of St Ia. The church was built in the early 15th century using granite quarried from sea-level cliffs near Zennor, a few miles west along the coast. The granite was carried by boat to St Ives.

THE PUTTING GREEN c1960 S22163

The putting green lies above Porthminster Beach. It was here, on rough sandy banks, that the St Ives pilchard fishing boats of the 19th century were drawn up clear of the beach. St Ives Station can be seen directly behind the boy in the foreground.

THE TREGENNA CASTLE HOTEL 1907 S22501

The Hotel has a fine cloak of ivy. Tregenna Castle is still one of St Ives' best known hotels, and now boasts a golf course amongst its many facilities.

Index

Frith Book Co 1999 Titles

From 2000 we aim at publishing 100 new books each year. For latest catalogue please contact Frith Book Co

Barnstaple	1-85937-084-5	£12.99	Oct 99
Blackpool	1-85937-049-7	£12.99	Sep 99
Bognor Regis	1-85937-055-1	£12.99	Sep 99
Bristol	1-85937-050-0	£12.99	Sep 99
Cambridge	1-85937-092-6	£12.99	Oct 99
Cambridgeshire	1-85937-086-1	£14.99	Nov 99
Cheshire	1-85937-045-4	£14.99	Sep 99
Chester	1-85937-090-X	£12.99	Nov 99
Chesterfield	1-85937-071-3	£12.99	Sep 99
Chichester	1-85937-089-6	£12.99	Nov 99
Cornwall	1-85937-054-3	£14.99	Sep 99
Cotswolds	1-85937-099-3	£14.99	Nov 99

Maidstone	1-85937-056-X	£12.99	Sep 99
Northumberland & Tyne and Wear	1-85937-072-1	£14.99	Sep 99
North Yorkshire	1-85937-048-9	£14.99	Sep 99
Nottingham	1-85937-060-8	£12.99	Sep 99
Oxfordshire	1-85937-076-4	£14.99	Oct 99
Penzance	1-85937-069-1	£12.99	Sep 99
Reading	1-85937-087-X	£12.99	Nov 99
St Ives	1-85937-068-3	£12.99	Sep 99
Salisbury	1-85937-091-8	£12.99	Nov 99
Scarborough	1-85937-104-3	£12.99	Sep 99
Scottish Castles	1-85937-077-2	£14.99	Oct 99
Sevenoaks and Tonbridge	1-85937-057-8	£12.99	Sep 99
Sheffield and S Yorkshire	1-85937-070-5	£12.99	Sep 99
Shropshire	1-85937-083-7	£14.99	Nov 99
Southampton	1-85937-088-8	£12.99	Nov 99
Staffordshire	1-85937-047-0	£14.99	Sep 99
Stratford upon Avon	1-85937-098-5	£12.99	Nov 99
Suffolk	1-85937-074-8	£14.99	Oct 99
Surrey	1-85937-081-0	£14.99	Oct 99
Torbay	1-85937-063-2	£12.99	Sep 99
Wiltshire	1-85937-053-5	£14.99	Sep 99

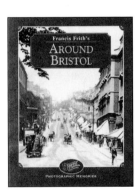

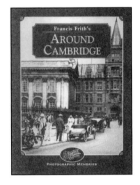

Derby	1-85937-046-2	£12.99	Sep 99
Devon	1-85937-052-7	£14.99	Sep 99
Dorset	1-85937-075-6	£14.99	Oct 99
Dorset Coast	1-85937-062-4	£14.99	Sep 99
Dublin	1-85937-058-6	£12.99	Sep 99
East Anglia	1-85937-059-4	£14.99	Sep 99
Eastbourne	1-85937-061-6	£12.99	Sep 99
English Castles	1-85937-078-0	£14.99	Oct 99
Essex	1-85937-082-9	£14.99	Nov 99
Falmouth	1-85937-066-7	£12.99	Sep 99
Hampshire	1-85937-064-0	£14.99	Sep 99
Hertfordshire	1-85937-079-9	£14.99	Nov 99
Isle of Man	1-85937-065-9	£14.99	Sep 99
Liverpool	1-85937-051-9	£12.99	Sep 99

British Life A Century Ago

246 x 189mm 144pp, hardback. Black and white Lavishly illustrated with photos from the turn of the century, and with extensive commentary. It offers a unique insight into the social history and heritage of bygone Britain.

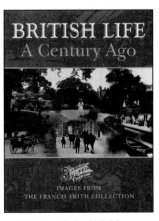

1-85937-103-5 £17.99

Available from your local bookshop or from the publisher

FRITH PRODUCTS & SERVICES

Francis Frith would doubtless be pleased to know that the pioneering publishing venture he started in 1860 still continues today. More than a hundred and thirty years later, The Francis Frith Collection continues in the same innovative tradition and is now one of the foremost publishers of vintage photographs in the world. Some of the current activities include:

Interior Decoration

Today Frith's photographs can be seen framed and as giant wall murals in thousands of pubs, restaurants, hotels, banks, retail stores and other public buildings throughout the country. In every case they enhance the unique local atmosphere of the places they depict and provide reminders of gentler days in an increasingly busy and frenetic world.

Product Promotions

Frith products have been used by many major companies to promote the sales of their own products or to reinforce their own history and heritage. Brands include Hovis bread, Courage beers, Scots Porage Oats, Colman's mustard, Cadbury's foods, Mellow Birds coffee, Dunhill pipe tobacco, Guinness, and Bulmer's Cider.

Genealogy and Family History

As the interest in family history and roots grows world-wide, more and more people are turning to Frith's photographs of Great Britain for images of the towns, villages and streets where their ancestors lived; and, of course, photographs of the churches and chapels where their ancestors were christened, married and buried are an essential part of every genealogy tree and family album.

A series of easy-to-use CD Roms is planned for publication, and an increasing number of Frith photographs will be able to be viewed on specialist genealogy sites. A growing range of Frith books will be available on CD.

The Internet

Already thousands of Frith photographs can be viewed and purchased on the internet. By the end of the year 2000 some 60,000 Frith photographs will be available on the internet. The number of sites is constantly expanding, each focussing on different products and services from the Collection.

Some of the sites are listed below.

www.townpages.co.uk
www.familystorehouse.com
www.britannia.com
www.icollector.com
www.barclaysquare.co.uk
www.cornwall-online.co.uk

For background information on the Collection look at the two following sites:

www.francisfrith.com
www.francisfrith.co.uk

Frith Products

All Frith photographs are available Framed or just as Mounted Prints, and can be ordered from the address below. From time to time other products - Address Books, Calendars, Table Mats, Postcards etc - are available.

The Frith Collectors' Guild

In response to the many customers who enjoy collecting Frith photographs we have created the Frith Collectors' Guild. Members are entitled to a range of benefits, including a regular magazine, special discounts and special limited edition products.

For further information: if you would like further information on any of the above aspects of the Frith business please contact us at the address below:
The Francis Frith Collection, Frith's Barn, Teffont, Salisbury, Wiltshire England SP3 5QP.
Tel: +44 (0) 1722 716 376 Fax: +44 (0) 1722 716 881 Email: frithbook.co.uk

To receive your FREE Mounted Print

Cut out this Voucher and return it with your remittance for £1.50 to cover postage and handling. Choose any photograph included in this book. Your SEPIA print will be A4 in size, and mounted in a cream mount with burgundy rule lines, overall size 14 x 11 inches.

Order additional Mounted Prints at HALF PRICE (only £7.49 each*)

If there are further pictures you would like to order, possibly as gifts for friends and family, acquire them at half price (no additional postage and handling required).

Have your Mounted Prints framed*

For an additional £14.95 per print you can have your chosen Mounted Print framed in an elegant polished wood and gilt moulding, overall size 16 x 13 inches (no additional postage and handling required).

---

* IMPORTANT!
These special prices are only available if ordered using the original voucher on this page (no copies permitted) and at the same time as your free Mounted Print, for delivery to the same address

---

Frith Collectors' Guild

From time to time we publish a magazine of news and stories about Frith photographs and further special offers of Frith products. If you would like 12 months FREE membership, please return this form and we will send you a New Member Pack.

Send completed forms to:
The Francis Frith Collection, Frith's Barn, Teffont, Salisbury, Wiltshire SP3 5QP

for FREE and Reduced Price Frith Prints

Picture no.	Page number	Qty	Mounted @ £7.49	Framed + £14.95	Total Cost
		1	**Free of charge***	£	£
			£	£	£
			£	£	£
			£	£	£
			£	£	£
			£	£	£
			* Post & handling		£1.50
			Total Order Cost		£

Title: AROUND PENZANCE

069-1

Please do not photocopy this voucher. Only the original is valid, so please cut it out and return it to us.

I enclose a cheque / postal order for £ . . . .
made payable to 'The Francis Frith Collection'
OR please debit my Mastercard / Visa / Switch / Amex card

Number . . . .

Expires . . . . Signature . . . .

Name Mr/Mrs/Ms . . . .

Address . . . .

. . . .

. . . .

. . . . Postcode . . . .

Daytime Tel No . . . .   Valid to 31/12/01

The Francis Frith Collectors' Guild

I would like to receive the New Members Pack offering 12 months FREE membership.

069-1

Name Mr/Mrs/Ms . . . .

Address . . . .

. . . .

. . . . Postcode . . . .

Free Print - see overleaf